IF I WERE TO SAY
SOMETHING ABOUT IT

STEFANIE GIDDENS

T.L. BIRCH
PUBLISHING INC

TL BIRCH
PUBLISHING INC

TL Birch Publishing Inc.
Kelowna, BC
Canada

If I were to say something about it by *Stefanie Giddens*
Copyright © 2024 by Stefanie Giddens
ISBN: 978-1-0689110-0-2 (paperback)
ISBN: 978-1-0689110-1-9 (ebook)

Photography by Darren Hull
Cover art and graphic design by Darcy Senger
Interior design by Jennifer Sparks, STOKE Publishing

For more information contact TL Birch Publishing Inc.
Email: info@tlbirch.com
Website: tlbirch.com

For all the women in shadows looking for light, for my mothers, my daughters, my granddaughter and all their fearlessness now and forever.

LAUREL

♡

Stefani

CONTENTS

INTRODUCTION

This is a book about love.

Just, not how you might expect.

It is a reconciliation. A witness of my life and the world around me. A path to my voice. And the search to find the one thing I wanted the most...to love myself.

And all these moments have shaped me, built me, broke me and saved me. There is no better or worse, just what was and what is.

More importantly, it is my reclamation as a woman. Speaking my truth as a woman. Defining these moments in a way that lets me let go.

After all the pain and suffering, there is love. Truly.

That's all.

So, is this a book about love? Yes, just not how you might expect.

I hope in these pages you find comfort in knowing you are not alone and there is light and love in darkness. Love is inside you, always.

Keep going. You are worth it.

Love, Me.

Trigger Warning

Some of the content in this book may be distressing for some readers.
There is an array of difficult themes, some of which are of emotional and sexual abuse, illness, death, loss and dysfunctional relationships.
Please read with care and seek support if needed.

PART ONE

I'm ok.

But, it has not always been that way.

I've spent my lifetime searching for worth, love and a voice of my own. It wasn't until I walked away from every expectation imposed on me by others and, more importantly, by myself that I began to find what I had been looking for all along.

I'm ok.

And *if I were to say something about it,* these would be the words that helped me see myself and the love I was looking for.

I Keep Going

He stood there
in front of me
grinning that boyish grin
the one that pulls you in
the one that says, "trust me"

And I do
Mesmerized by the glint in his eyes
his boyish ways
my burn to please

Please pick me
Please treat me right
Please show me you care
Please know how much I try
Please give me a crumb of your stare
Please, please, please
see me

Every effort is lost
swallowed up in his insatiable need
to be right
To be on the edge of being someone
he can never be
To manipulate his way through
my weakness
Until I only know his truth

I am his mirror
built over a decade or more
Of lies
Of deceit
Of stealing
Of not seeing

Because truth is expensive
It comes with the price tag of excommunication
Rejection
And seven years of bad luck
Weakness leveraged
for all I have earned
smashed at my feet

He listens and smiles
Yet knows not of the depth
of a woman
beaten with her own loyalty, faith and goodwill
And the notes I have taken
he doesn't see it coming

I chuckle at his empty stare
nod at his words of praise that no longer resonate
And slowly
I smile
my biggest reflective, boyish grin
Umm hmmm, yes, I know
trust me

Tea Leaves

There are seventeen ways to die
she said
I only know of four
she continued

The first one
is to stop loving.

The second one
to stop loving yourself.

The third
give up.

And the fourth…

Stop believing in magic.

I have never done any of these
She said
That is why I will live on
and
She continued

Pain

You've haunted me for so long
That soft subtle ache
around my heart
The sharp edge
worn down over many years
with forgiveness
compassion
understanding
belief and tears

But it doesn't take much
to grind the blunt edge
sharp again
with fear

That I will never be enough

To stand up against you

When I am alone
my dreams matter
When I am alone
I am everything
and more

But all it takes
is the hint of your apparition
The slam of a door
that was never open

to remind me of how far I have come
And how far I have yet to go

And that slow gentle squeeze
around my heart
The pressing weight of disbelief

The memory of heat
and softness
The searing edge that divides me

Between now or never
Between you or me

For as much as you will always haunt me
I will eventually
see right through you
Use you
But never
be terrorized
by your sharp edge

How Dare You

How dare you say
"It was only___"
"It was just___"
"Others have it worse"

The sharpness of those words
tumbled long enough
around in your mouth
on your tongue
to become polished and smooth
Harmless
Soften the edges
that sliced
the innocence
from me
when I wasn't looking
When trust was free

How I long to go back
and scream
at the top of my lungs
so all the neighbours
could hear
So I was the last
So that all the men
I endured
treated me better

But perhaps
you are right
The sharpness of it all
could be smoother
if I dare say it enough

"It was only my innocence"
"It was just my childhood"
"Others have it worse"

Slow Burn

My tongue
touched
metal
in the cold
dark
places
of my life
where
I couldn't say a word
Because
I couldn't find it

I was stuck
Frozen
And I clamped down hard
to keep
a measure
of reality
with me
For fear
of losing myself
in a winter storm

I sunk
my teeth
into my tragedy
for I thought
somewhere

in all this sorrow
I would find
comfort

But all it did
was
debride my growth
My way out

Metal
has a distinct
taste
It's bitter
It's something you
never forget
Like the smell
of blood

I wanted to
taste
the
fruits of my labours
the softness
of skin
and shiver
from the
fear

of heights
of the tower
they had put
me in

I wanted
to fall
freely
whole heartedly
with
a soft bend
in my back
an
archway
into my
future
A drop
from darkness

And I went
from
metal to glass
Still stuck
with a view
and the words
Because I had found them
along the way

but
they were words
no one
wanted to hear

And even though
it was
light
and

bright
with so much promise
all I could
think of
was
the darkness
and
my tongue
touching metal
and
the searing pain
of
the words
that set me free
from
the winter

The metal
that
trapped me in glass
and
the years
I believed
it was

Different

Better

Until I found myself
walking
for miles
on the shards
of all I had built

The fruits of
my labours
A kind of
leeching of them
and their
inappropriate
words
touches
smiles

I felt myself slipping
And there was a distant smell
One you never forget

If I fell
the metal
would have no bend
and
I would taste it
Forever

As I licked
my wounds
from the long miles
I tasted something
Primal

Something
I now know
they all feared

Something
they tried to
get rid of

But once you get
a taste
there's no going back

It's an elixir
already inside you
A serum
that flows through you

The drops
on my tongue
set my senses on fire
and I grew
bigger than I ever had before

And I trembled
Arched my back
with arms outstretched
to the sky
and I reached up
staring straight
into the sun
Everything burned

And I rose up
better than Jesus

For the first time
I truly saw
Myself
reflected
in the
metal and glass

Dangerous Dreaming

What if
all the women
in the world
All quit
at the same time
Just

Quit

What if they
broke away from
Conventions
Self doubt
Second best
Less than
Being told (rather than heard)

What if
we became

Shapeless
Borderless
Powerful
Free

What if
at the same time
Every
Single
Woman
had the same thought

I quit

The Man

Why is it that
you so badly
want me to be
a man?

Powerful
Strong
Independent
Tough

The list of power words
is long

But, again
Why is it that
you so badly
want me to be
a man?

When
I am already
all the things
you want me
to be
mixed in all
my layers
of complexity

Beauty
Tenderness
Kindness
And
Sensuality

Why is it
you want me
to bring
Aggression
Fear
And
Intimidation
to those in
my care
When as a
Woman
it is the tenderness
of my
weakness
that makes me
reject the notions
of ever becoming a man

The Reclamation

It's like digging for a sliver
buried deep in your flesh

It hurts
but
you can't find it

It's festering madness
pain
and
irritation

You know it's there
But
Try to ignore it
Every time you
wrap your arms
around someone
it pokes at you
Sends
a flash of pain
that makes you
retreat

I'm no expert
at extracting
slivers
even though I have many

But I am good
at pretending
they're not there
An expert
at pain

I want to believe
that
others put them in me
But
Truth is…
They never slid my soul
against the
cedar railing

I did.

And I have found
those shards
to be helpful
To help me be
Sick
and
Tired

To help me be
Infectious

But it is time
I work on
my wounds
Soak in salt water
to draw out
the disintegrated
memories
and
cellular debris

Time to heal
Time to be

And as I begin
to mine the layers
with sight
and sound
I realize
love does not rush in
from the
outside
to fill the spaces
carved out by
history
and
subtle violence
Yes, it helps

But

The elixir
is
Love
from
the
Inside
Out
radiating into
the world
Personal sunshine
and lollipops

I shall no longer
lick my wounds
with shame and darkness
I will sing
Like a Goddess
Stitched up
with the words
of
Her Story

PART TWO

I wasn't always ok.

In fact, there were times I toyed with the burn of a razor on my flesh, line after line of red down my arms. Another time when I wanted the pain to go away so badly that I found myself in an ER room bleeding and in tears. Because I had been made to feel worthless. Because I was betrayed. Because I was too young to understand I could say no.

But, there was something deep inside of me that would not let the pain win.

I kept going.

And *if I were to say something about it*, these would be the words of things I could never speak about.

Destruction

There was a beauty only she could see
And when she started to speak of it
they grew angry
Showed their teeth
Told her she was
a god dammed liar
And chased her
until
she could run no more
And she lay at
their feet
for them to scoop her up
tie her to a stake and burn her
For all they saw
was her light in their darkness
And she wailed in the moonlight
as the flames rose
the pain
the suffering
all she had endured
for speaking of
beauty
something only she saw
and they never would
And as they picked at her bones
as the ashes smouldered
there was a howl
a sigh

and a cry
stronger than they had ever heard in the night
as the night birds
screeched
and pierced their hearts
with shame
for what they had done
to one of the most
beautiful things
in the world.

The Tipping Point

Those who will survive
are the ones
who give up the past
and put it behind them

Those were the words
that dripped off his lips
Spoken in defiance
and trained
ignorance

For there was destruction all around
unacknowledged
scoffed at
Realities met
with the privilege
of not being
a woman

A woman
broken into many pieces
they could use
Could sell
Or just
toy with
for their pure enjoyment

She was theirs to break
because they could
because they can

But
it is those who can leave the past
behind
who will
survive them

Shame

I just picked my nose.
Trying to sort out where to smear the sticky bit as his hand
expertly slides up my leg and into my pants.

I panic.

How embarrassing it would have been for him to see the
booger. I hide it. Wipe it on the edge of the camper mattress and
quickly get rid of
the evidence.

I'm not sure what I think of his hand,
but I like his dog - the one his girlfriend bought
and I reach out to the dog as a distraction.
She licks me and it tickles.

'Down there' it kind of tickles too as his fingers find the moist
and slippery spot that makes me a girl. He lets me walk the dog,
cut the lawn, make bullets downstairs and lay on the couch
with him.

He's done this before.
We play cards, and he cooks me lunch. Sometimes his girlfriend
comes over and then it's not as much fun, so I usually walk
across the street and play in my own yard.

Trouble is,
he has better trees to climb. Some of them even grow cherries
and I like to sit in the tree and eat as many as I can

before I get caught.
I don't like getting caught. I don't like getting in trouble. It gives me a tummy ache, so I listen, I behave and I do as I'm told.

I'm a good girl.

He's really nice to me and one of my favourite things to do is to go for a motorbike ride down to Rose's store for a bottle of pop. He gets his big motorbike out and I get a helmet on. Mom helps me to make sure it is on right, so I am safe and then off we go. I wave to mom and sometimes dad with a big smile on my face, giddy for an adventure.

But, I don't like it so much when he shows me pictures of naked women. The pictures his brother took of all his girlfriends, saved in a box in the upstairs bedroom.

I think those pictures are dumb and those girls are stupid. When I'm naked, I make sure no one sees me. After my bath at night my mom wraps me in a towel and I run as best I can up the stairs before my brother sees me and calls after me, "Chicken legs! You have chicken legs!"
The only naked picture of me is the one in the bath when I was, like, one and you can't even see anything. I mean, like, whatever, they're just nipples. Not like now where I'm pretty sure any day now I'll be sprouting boobies. I hope.

Hopefully, they won't look like those girls in the pictures. They don't have very big ones, and I'm gonna have big boobs. And when I am in grade six, mom says I can get my ears pierced. I didn't see any earrings on the naked girls.

So
there.

I can't go across the street to his house today. She's there and he told me they are trying to make a baby.
They will be making love.
I don't know why they would want to make a baby just yet. I don't quite get it because

they're not even married.

But, I can't even go over there, so I wander around, bored, wishing I could mow the lawn or eat cherries.

Sometimes I get really bored over there. Especially after lunch when he lays on the couch and watches TV.
Lots of times I lay on the floor, but most of the time I lay on the couch
then his hands pull me close to his body and move wherever they want to.

My underpants sometimes get really wet and gooey and I don't know why.

And some other times my pants are a bit too tight and there is
not enough room for my tummy with his hand down there.
So,
mostly,
I just wiggle around a bit to make myself more comfortable.
And, I change the channels when he does it - his hands can't do
both, so I get the controller.

This stuff didn't happen when his mom lived there and he came
to visit her.
We would all sit around the table and chat. She always had a
cookie or home baked treats for me.

She moved out of the house and he moved in.
That's when the visits changed, but I didn't want to be a bad
guest– a bad girl, so I listen, I do what I'm told, obey and I let
my mind wander.

My imagination is really good. I go all sorts of places when he
traps me on a bed upstairs, on a bunk bed in the basement
against the panel board wall, in the garage or the back porch
with the ivy all around. The garden shed, the camper, the
kitchen, the car.

Mom and dad asked me once, "Does he touch you?"
I pretended he didn't, so nothing really happened. "Nope, what
are you talking about? He's really nice to me." That was that.

And it never came up again.

It's been years since he moved away. He got married, and they moved up north.
I didn't go over much after he got married.
And I said a brief goodbye to them, the day they left – the same day I got my ears pierced.

I was in a lot of pain.
My ears hurt and he was leaving.

I never saw him in person again. Just in pictures every Christmas.
Him, her
and eventually, his two daughters.

It's been a long road of memories, a long summer of remembering a forever's length of pain.

The cheap panel board,
the sound of plastic storage bags rustling as I scrambled to move away.
The goofy antics I tried to escape his preying eyes, and his wandering hands.
The smell of gunpowder and the open door to the next room, the camper and the words I could never put together.
Every moment never left me, every touch, every breath, every lunch, every card game and all those naked girls.

Yes, the girls I left behind.
The dog,
the wife,
the pictures
and me.
All girls swallowed up by slippery touches, expert hands and
cherries that needed picking in the tree.

The girls I couldn't save arrived every Christmas.

Because I couldn't find the words, I couldn't open doors in a
house that didn't belong to me.

The little girls in pictures are in a box upstairs in the attic.
Waiting,
waiting,
waiting
and waiting
for me to finally put the words together.

No, no, no!

Blindsided

It was you
who consumed the flesh
of peasant girls

Who followed in your father's footsteps
and stole
the next generation of trust
Then left

You spoke of false promises
Under the guise
of
your parents' wishes

The talk of marriage
was a ruse
to swoon
the peasant girls
you preyed upon

The hope of elevation
to a good life
A handsome husband
The envy
of
all the girls

A summer burn
that lingered like poison
And killed
all the joy
from my memory
of us
As children

A poison
that leached into
all the happy
days
When I trusted you
When we ran free
in endless hot days

But I was always
just a peasant girl
who was
oblivious
to your taking

And just like our happy days
it ended with the night

As you compared
notes with your father
making sure

we were all
crossed off
I hope beside my name
was those
of your future daughters
Names you'll recognize
on someone else's list

And as you watch them cry with heartache
you will remember
the days
when you preyed on
Peasant girls

To my abuser

If you were to ever stand in front of me
again
I would just have one question

Was it worth it?

Faith

I was raised on it
Spoonful by spoonful
A fundamental requisite for rearing a child
in that day and age
Full fat milk, no eggs
Only sweet nectar of incantations, chants and creeds I came
to love
The familiar melody of prayers and songs with God and birds
I gulped it down without question
I grew exactly how I was supposed to
Carried the weight of holy responsibility straight as a
wooden beam
Until
Razor thin cuts dropped me to my knees
Cut after cut
Burning I could not bear anymore with no answer in the dark as
I wept with shadows
Every fiber that knit the fabric of my existence
Unraveled
And the long string of spirit pulled me away from all I knew
I ran to the outreaches of freedom
I threw myself at unknown causes to hear my heart beat
I fell down hills
At the bottom I rested on a bruised and thin scarred reality
Tired
Faith is the very thing that dissected my heart, spun my soul
and darned the holes in my endless universe with it
Faith is the very thing that has slammed me into my reflection
laughing

It indignantly states, "You don't know what the fuck you
believe, do you?"
I scream, I laugh and I swallow tall glasses of uncertainty
It is not what I was raised on, spoonful by spoonful
but everything I have spit out
that has stopped the razors, the spoons and the sweet nectar
from burying me under who everyone wants me to be and
books that say I should be something more than what I
already am.

PART THREE

Love can be messy and I seemed to find my fair share of chaos and broken hearts. Whether I was reckless with my heart or others, I was trying to be what I thought others wanted me to be and failing miserably. I wanted to be saved, never realizing that only I could save myself.

But, I kept going. Kept trying to figure it out.

Until I started to love myself, it was difficult to find love in another.

And *if I were to say something about it*, these would be the words of broken hearts and falling in and out of love.

Penance

She stood at the edge of the ocean
searching for something
she could not have
the ache for a lover
that would not come

She breathed in the salt air
sweat trickled down her brow
as the waves crashed in
washing over her
one
at a time

She was alone

But all was beautiful around her
she had what everyone wanted
well, almost
everything
(but that was her secret)

Diamonds sparkled on the ocean
the waves
heaved all day
and her expectations
were as steady as the waves
leaving her

Alone

One at a time
at the edge of the ocean

I think his name started with G

Had I known you were going to die so young
perhaps
I might have loved you
just a little longer

But, you wished to possess me
hang onto me
when my wildness
could not
allow
any permanence
any caring
any
love

And you so desperately
wanted love
All the things I could not give
because
I was in no state
to even give them to myself

I was in the middle of
destruction
You fell in my path
too early
too soon
too softly

So, all I could do
was consume the parts of you
I wanted
and then
just
leave

I am desperately sorry
you ended so soon
that your wife was left
broken hearted and alone
that
I
broke off a piece of you
like candy

It really was just one night of dancing
and a narrow miss
of being broken and alone

All the things I never said

Spoken words failing to become public have drowned out the whispers of realism in my mind.

I am a romantic.
An odd romantic of sorts.

Not the novel sort or the kind that you would find in the pages of a textbook. No, I am on an odyssey of my own. My own romantic quest.

Questioning and becoming.
If nothing else, a misunderstood Misses or Ms.
The counterbalance of my femininity against my insatiable emotional drama has dropped me into a tide of perpetual loneliness.

The sea is a lonely place to sail alone.

It's the constant pull of humanness, kindness, desperation that gravitates me to the eddying, emotionally damaged maleness. They are cute, two-dimensional paper ken dolls waiting to be dressed or undressed.

Depends on perspective.

They are the men I love. They are the men I hate.

Some days, I'm not sure where the border exists between the two.

What is real, what is perceived and what is next.

I didn't want to bring this up; commitment.
Never with me. I fight it too much. Perhaps the wrong way. A
poorly constructed battle.

But, the future ex-girlfriends and the former ex-girlfriends seem
to manage the duo, the partnering with Mr. Ken. And I wonder.
Is it co-dependent in nature, or merely that they have found a
better cheerleader for their favourite person? Their mirror's
reflection.

The reflection I used to be. To worship.

What does this say about me? I've had various responses. The
latest was the most revealing. "You are fucked up beyond all
reason – good luck with that." The acronym is FUBAR. (I
wonder if it spells any other words? Probably not.) Even if it
did it really doesn't fit into my romantic notions.

Little words of love.
Jaded love.
Mistaken text.
Miss taken.

Feminist fool. Man hater. Satan worshiper. (Only if he was
female though.) Word creator for little girls. Created text
unclaimed in the mist of youth. Unchained thoughts furrowing
into the fertile minds of future women.

Stopped.
Slammed into barriers put up by Father Ken.

It's the shifting of the metaphysical that makes it all so unfair.
But, who said it would be when you were sold on an idea?

Ideals.

Doubting.
Giving the benefit of the doubt.
Creating an even playing field. (In all fairness, of course.)

I have lashed out. I know how to push buttons. Commit havoc.
Verbal treason in a trial of emotion. Linguistic flooding
negatively charged and received.

Implications of forbidden subjects.
For a reaction.
That's all.

I'll get what I want if I really, really try. You can't just depend
on "fuck you" anymore. It has to be bigger. Less social.
Underused and personally incorrect. It must get to the heart of
the matter.

Politically speaking, of course.

It's inevitable that they come back. Ken dolls with new Barbies.
Cheering and smiling.

Maybe that's the problem – they thought I was Barbie.

Laugh, cry and then try hard to drink it away. Anything medicinal helps. Substance abuse.

I'm not Barbie.
Or I would still be with all the paper dolls.
The broken boys dressing to get undressed.

It's the violence of love in learning something foreign. The not falling. Just feeling and exploring.

Sex.

It's really better with two people. I've heard stories about more than two, but that leads me into a religious, moralistic, existentialist debate that I have not had the time to reconcile. Internal confusion leaves me comfortable with the opposite gender.

One at a time.

I have always thought about sex as the ultimate motion of love. If love was finding a way to express, it would be in making it.

One body fitting neatly into another.
Like hands clasping on a sunny walk together.
In a park by the sea.

Open. Longing to find the deepest parts. The strong tides of emotions that need to not be spoken. Silence to a degree is all that is. The motions of nature reverberate between two bodies growing together. Flesh on flesh.

I'm lost in thought and may never come back to the surface. I like it here. It is where I can play out all the cruel things I never did. All the romantic things I wish had happened. I can make him want me, take me away and seduce me. I can make him real.

Really.
He wants me.

I've always wanted someone to want me. And so I linger in the demi-conscious. My mind creates the safe place to remember him and them. I loved them all, but I have yet to fall in love with anyone.

There is a difference.
You know.

I'm waiting for peace and an end to relational destruction. Because in the end there is no blame. Just perspective. How we see. The experience stays. So pretty, so poised, so perfect yet trapped.

That's the conceived problem. Feeling trapped. Like there is nothing that can be done. Nothing to do.

But reconciliation is partly textual.
The other is verbal.

I'm not out of my mind yet. I will be. Soon. I'm just waiting.

Waiting to say,
all the things I never said.

Love next door

Many nights
in lucid splendor
kept me with you
Each day
harboured the longing for
another night
Nothing but darkness
Silence
Only the sound of
night and love

Riddled Explanations

I reached out my hand
Said Hello
It was the seed in the garden
Ready
Wanting to grow.

Everything was rich
Thick with passion
Ready

Twelve days passed
Twelve weeks
Our hours were tangled
Deeper

Stable plans were made
Roots discussed
Futures in the making
Truly

A wind blew
An emotional eclipse
No sun or reason

Violent
Broken plants
Metal rods and sharp edges
Cutting marks and remarks

Still,
I question it all.

A thin straight line of love

A thin straight line of love
has ripped them in two
Fame laces up the wound
while ghosts escape like smoke through teeth.

The razor like passion
slides up and down wires
Sounds of a pent up high
screaming a chorus that never ends at night.

They drift in and out
never the same twice
Always new with dawn
when all that burns is the ghost that escaped.

It comes in waves
crashing with soft currents
Dreams so quiet
with the flash of lights and jagged promises.

In two pieces
an endless struggle
Back and forth
with always wanting and the stillness inside.

Betrayal

I'm not sure what I like more, making you suffer, the fight, or the pain I caused when I slept with your boyfriend.

I severed our friendship on a winter night while you waited for him to come home, instead his hands were in mine while the snow fell from the sky and silenced our passion.

So many days had passed from the moment we met. Buried inside my first hello to him was 'I will have you'. And so began our journey of silent attraction, of deception and dangerous hellos.

You, yes you. I had never much liked you, but the time came that I needed you, so I put on my best friend face and played the game. I think you idolized me. And, I liked it. But not really you. You had a soft pathetic way about you that tricked people. But I knew what you were up to. I could see behind the mousey stare, the twitchy little nose that wiggled its way into other peoples' business. The secrets you discovered and hoarded away. Your security deposit on friendships you were never capable of.

I saw beyond the veil of pathetic and weak. The acts of kindness that got you closer to what you wanted – an image to be more than what you were. Coattails to ride on. Waters to muddy with your dirty lies and grimy secrets.

Funny how you always seemed to have the same past as everyone else.

You lacked the sharpness of truth, the melancholy of yesterday and the sting of reality. You rode on fantasy, contradiction, and the personality of vanilla. Even the Swiss chocolate you brought back for me could not coat your words in velvet.

Maybe it was the night you undressed me and washed your eyes over me. You turned the lights out and hesitated for a very long time. A hesitation just about as long as the man who loved me in my nineteenth year.

He knew it was wrong, but my young body, in his bed, in a cabin by the lake with the guilt of his age washed away with Grand Marnier he knelt by the bed contemplating his next move. I was so scared. Not because of him, but because of me. Looking back, I know he loved me, but I wasn't very good at saying what I meant without the contrast of yes and no. I lived in absolutes. He almost forty – everything around me said no even though my spirit begged for yes.

You hesitated just like him.

I heard you breathing, wanting something out of the darkness that I could never give. Hesitation is a matrix of problems and solutions. There are no answers inside it, just next steps that determine your path. And either way, you have failed and succeeded – ignored the conventions of universal laws and robbed yourself of destiny in one considerable moment that questioned intuition.

In his hesitation, I realized we were more than just friends.

In your hesitation, I realized how much I wanted you gone. How much disgust and malevolence I felt for you.

Get out!

Your hesitation was a razor blade that started its journey through several layers of friendship and got down to the raw reality of my burning desire to sever you from my mind.

Get out bitch!

You fucking pathetic loser, go!

My rage burned in the darkness. Even the alcohol couldn't mask the poison seeping into the night. Get out.

And I breathed in and out a poison that could not leave the room. It trailed out of the room when you finally left because you thought I was sleeping. I may have staggered up the stairs to my bedroom in an uninhibited state of whiskey moments, but I walked purposely down those same stairs to lock you out of my life.

Your car started, I heard you leave – the sound of poison dragging behind you.

The air cleared.

Deception always lies on both sides of the fence and in the middle, we try to hurdle over hate. To get past the betrayal. To get beyond the reality of what just happened.

You let it happen and so did I.

The only way you could ever be with me was through him. Your vanilla soul, the handmaid's stare and the mousey twitch of emotions melted on him like the snowflakes on that winter's night that made up for all those moments you wanted so badly to touch me and all you could do was hesitate, beg him for love and watch me melt into his hands.

The love of a pigeon

Her begging heart is cracked
like endless sidewalks
resting on steam grates
waiting for the day to end
and the night to cover up her sorrow
She sleeps
Executive grins walk past her
look down on her
Managed looks of judgement
No one stops with quarters
No pennies for her thoughts
But around her
they protect her from glances
The serenade of distraction
The shimmering feathered song
One that struts in the sun
Colored
Puffed
She sleeps while he proudly coos around her
And the flock
loves her
on the sidewalk

Stranger on the dance floor

There is a hole in the wall
from last night
when rage and jealousy found its way home
Drywall still crumbles
bits of love on the floor

"What the fuck were you doing?"

I wasn't doing any thing
His hands were
and you saw
It
All

"Where were you??"

He was outside escaping the black-tie affair
Talking to buddy
about nothing
Laughing
instead of
Protecting
Me

"Don't tell me you couldn't feel his hands all over you!"

I will tell you that all day long, love
Because

I was frozen all over
Haunted by
hands
that didn't belong
where
they
were

None of any things
should have happened

I have to sweep up the drywall, deal with it

Who will fix this hole?

Strength

Driving in my car, eyes straight ahead. Piercing the future through hot tears.

I'm so fucking mad right now.

The blame is 10 miles behind me, but it rides with me as I navigate the road.

I've been here before. Seventeen miles from somewhere, getting nowhere.

Why do I let him do this to me? The hurls of, "You did this, you don't do that…" The 'shoulds' of yesterday the 'woulds' of today.

Fuck it then.

I won't go.
I won't stay.
I won't worry about myself.
I'll shut up and stay miserable in the noise of not saying anything.
I'll behave.
I'll live in a box.
I'll fit perfectly into the mold of what he wants me to be.

Ya, that's what l'll do. I'll show him how square I can be, caged up like a blue crested bird that only sings for him.

But, there's something that doesn't let me win with my empty promises. There's something behind the hot tears and the steering wheel that navigates nowhere.

It's the song that I sing only for me with no lock, no key and no cage.

It's the road less travelled that takes me only where I want to go regardless of a, "Fuck you!" or a "You're not."
It's a path I have built with every doubt, placed with moments of pain, moments of joy and the sheer will to just keep going.
Even after slamming doors, miles of tears and roads that lead nowhere, it always leads me home.
Where I can rest on the soft sorrow and the strength of tomorrow.

Intimacy

I'm not sure I love him anymore.

Perhaps it is the any part.
Perhaps it is the more.

What more is there when I'm tied up in his expectations?

I need a softer touch, spoon-fed velvet handfuls of love.
Soft kissing words.
Wet lips tattooed on my skin from head to toe.
Anything other than the bonds thrust upon me that tie me up
with the searing sting of barbed wire cuts. Cuts that fester with
ignorance and neglect. The small cuts any can make, if you
love it.

Oh but the rush of it, wave after wave of love and hate, hate and
love, it channels me to a state of poisoned kindness.

I really love you. Anymore.

And our chaos of give and take of a thousand cuts bleeding
promises maybe next time. I'm sorry.
Maybe next time I'll come to a place of understanding your
hard love as it lays on me with pleasure. As it strikes me with
fear and incompetence in the soft velvet handful of love forced
down my throat.

I don't love you anymore.
I love you now.

In the moment you hurt me rushing into an argument that
steams up the windows with shame.
I'm so close to you in the pain, in the cuts and the sweetness of
your infectious love.

It's the sliver I can't get out of my system.

And around my finger, the golden bond that reminds me of our
adventure through the heaves of years and the ecstasy of
tomorrow.

I don't love you any.
I don't love you more.

Clarity

An expectation
unforgiven and forgotten
at the end of what was love
Misunderstood reasons
Misunderstood rhetoric
Aching reality
spreads into tomorrow
Clarity
is lost
Smeared across the assumption
that I feel
for you.

Midnight Rain

The painful moments
are the ones
when you are
alone

When no one
is in them
with you

That's when
he touches me

When I am aching
broken
and
lonely in the rain

When the light sleeps
and I can't

He touches me
so I can
rest
so he can hold my pain
in the darkness
when it rains

PART FOUR

Loss has been no stranger to me.

I took my first steps the day of my grandfather's funeral, so it's no surprise that death would be part of the big learnings in my life. It never gets easier the more you encounter it, but you understand something deeper, delicate and possibly pre-destined about our time here.

I have lost many and witnessed others as they have grappled with loss.

It has changed me. And will continue to.

But, we must keep going. Love deeply. Live greatly. End well.

And *if I were to say something about it*, these would be the words of grief, sadness, honour and loss.

Suicide

I stare down at three hours of violence.
The blood slowly creeps towards my feet wanting me to
become part of the tragedy and history that will never wash out
with soap and water.

As I look down into his dead eyes, I look for some small sign of
hope - some reason to hurry, but there is nothing except the
remnants of terror and anguish lying motionless on the tarmac
six hours from where his once happy life shattered.

I struggle to find my place in this mess. I've never liked guns
and here I am twenty-one years old sorting out the taste of a
shotgun in a small northern town.

Who does this and why?

Part of the answer, the first part, is right in front of me and my
young mind can't quite pull all the pieces together. The blood,
the gun, the truck with the engine still running, the empty face
and me, frozen in confusion, frozen in understanding of a life
gone with the pull of a trigger.

Bang, you're dead.

The answer to 'why' I'm sure, will linger for the many years
ahead. The answer gone with one shell deployed from
desperation and despair of loss. The scattered fragments of why
placed in his home, broken by leaving love, children taken and
a wife in hiding.

Scattered on the highway as he drove to find them, on the doorsteps of neighbours when he screamed, "Where is she?!!" More pieces in the truck he drove following the school bus his children were riding in, waving to him and the bus driver that wouldn't stop.

And then the final bits traveled with the heavy weight of sadness, hopelessness, and a shotgun, down an unused road to the tarmac, to the moment where 'why' didn't matter anymore…only now and them and love.

A mind torn in three.
One for her, one for him and one for them.

There were no tender kisses on his cheek, no passion on his lips, no arms around him as he died. No one but the wind that carried the kisses from the bus, the sky that was his blanket and the asphalt that was his bed.

The sun had left him too. Scared by the thoughts of things to come, the knowing of what was about to happen and the things that did. Only a dull grey light cast down on the scene and me. Detached and struggling, not only with the weight of death and a body with no pulse, but of what the sun was hiding from.

Knowing.

Knowing the face of a man I didn't know would be burnt in my mind. His story bit by bit would find me and piece by piece, the tragedy would come together to the place I stood with the blood creeping towards me. His face still there and still here.

And when the moon is full, the stars alive, and the night rushing past, I can still see his face staring into the sky.

There is not much time or space or sunshine to take away the grey memories, the pain and the three hours of violence I carried away in a small northern town, where the taste of a shotgun and the stretch of the tarmac lead only to questions that will never be answered.

Constant directions

Green arrows and lights point
They tell me to go
and in what direction.

But I wander

Futile are the efforts to find a path
for there are none etched in emotions

How do you map out death?
When do you get over loss?

Get over it.
Move past it.
Move on.

I'm moving
everywhere
and I see nothing but darkness
and fear

I ache for reason
for a moment of caring that lasts
into tomorrow

Out over the meadow that reaches tomorrow
I'm looking for a giant arrow that says
You are here
Now.

Separation

I looked at her and into her deep half-moon eyes.
The words had been spoken, "I'm leaving."
And my heart knew.
It knew of the pain, the loss, the sadness and the ache of a lost
boy who can't come home.
So, she's leaving
To find her Kurtz a whole world away.
There is something about leaving that frees you
helps you let go and get out of the way of yourself.

The clouds are dark in her half-moon eyes. Searching for
daylight, the reflection of water and the validity of someone's
record to say,
you were here.
She is in my heart
But, she is leaving.

And as I sit there staring into the storm
I see my mother.
I see the pull of the future
and the weight of the past, both firmly anchored in today
She is leaving.

I guess I knew, maybe before she did
There was a great pain, an enduring sadness that sat right
behind her smile.
She wears the years on her face.

The lines written on the soft texture of skin.
Scars of the past smoothed out with lotion
in the morning.

She touches me
and it's as if God has breathed down on me
whispering
"Keep going, it will be ok."

But, where were the soft touches when the devil was at her
door?
Where was the comfort of loving arms, tender kisses or
the courage of commitment?
It was next door
Down the street
Spilling off of tables and clattering onto the floor.

It was wasted.

Betrayed.

Gone.

And I pray for her. I pray for a witness to nurture her heart
through the sorrows.
To bring her life.
To bring greater fullness.

She is leaving.

I listen as her half-moon eyes fill with seventeen years of
sorrow
and day by day
trickle down her cheek.
There is no room for error as I witness a wound rubbed raw
with salt.

And she tells me of the world she knew
Of the children at play
Of their moon beam laughter
Their dark skin
And the road she must travel to get back to them.

We wind through the mountains,
the journey that has spilt us
the moment that came from snow-capped mountains
half moons
dark skin and laughter

She is leaving.
To Africa
To innocence
And to a childhood of moon beam laughter
And a dark continent of love.

She is leaving
She is leaving
She is
leaving me

Lip Gloss

As I flopped down in bed after a long day of particular children wanting little bits of me at every turn, I realize the dryness and monotony of the day has ended up on my lips, as I purse them together in the last frays of the day.

One more time, I have to sit up and get something for myself even though it is a short hand reach away in my night table.

Mothers never stop the getting, the giving, the fetching, the helping...the everything that the torrents of the day-to-day froth around them. In the midst of swirling hours sometimes the glancing moment to dip one's finger in a coin-sized container of tangerine lip gloss, press the substance on parched skin lips one at a time and feel the sheer texture of clear smelly bliss wipe away the dryness of the day as one lip slides against the other, is all a pulled mother needs to endure just one more tenacious event.

But, it's eleven o'clock and I'm tired.

I just need the lip gloss in my nightstand to prevent cracking, bleeding, hard-to-heal sores from forming on my lips.

I suppose it's partly the weather, a lack of water and me not giving a dam about some beauty product regime that has made my kissers this way.

At thirty, I was supposed to get on board with the cosmetic regime, but thirty is too far away from forty to care about eternal youth…thirty is also too close to twenty-five to think that you are 'old' or 'over the hill' and now at thirty-four, I am wishing I was forty so that I had an excuse for the age that has accumulated on my face over the last few years.

Lip gloss.

I reach over to the unfinished wooden nightstand (a woodworking project eternally on the go with no definite finish date or time), pull open the drawer and rustle around in the disarray of odds and ends.

Price tags, grocery receipts, hair ties, trinkets, notes, letters and a few saved cards form a collage of reminders – things I have to do and things I have done. There are also things that cannot wait like lip gloss and him.

The wallet size picture of his face surfaces with my rooting around and I stop. Staring down, I retrieve it from the chaos of my nightstand drawer.

The memory of lip gloss has left my mind.

My husband rouses from his snoring slumber, looking up at me with heavy lids, he mumbles something about it being late, the light and work in the morning, then rolls over and blocks all chances of a nighttime embrace with a wall of his wide shoulders and strong back.

I look down at the palm sized picture in my hand.

It wasn't that long ago that he was larger than life. At least to me he was. A mosaic of moments floods my mind, but one comes into focus and I rest my thoughts there.

He was standing precariously on a section of chopped firewood, propped up vertically on the beach. It resembled a topless tree buried in the sand neck deep by a group of mischievous kids.

He wasn't a big man, but he was tall, lanky and thin.
He was one of those young men you couldn't quite judge when it came to strength.
His looks were unsuspecting, but there was an undercurrent that discouraged trouble.

He wasn't the violent or aggressive sort anyway. Most of his seriousness and male conjecture was part of his exquisite delivery of unending jokes.

Oh how he made us laugh.

It wasn't so much the joke, but the anticipation of how he would act out each phrase, say each line with all the right inflection points or emphasis and how he would contort his face into each character's emotion.
He was better than good and could have made a living making people laugh, but he opted for other paths and adventures.

So did fate.

As he stood on that log buried in the beach, the fire licked at his shadow, lighting up the small crowd of friends that had joined together for a night under the stars. The night was quiet except for the crackle of the fire, his voice and the howls as we doubled over in an overabundance of his ability to make us laugh 'til we hurt.

One day I will attempt his Two Guns joke he was so well known for.
But, not now. Not right now.

I smile just a little at the warm memory of long ago days, good friends and him.
The brief moment and movement of dry lips splits my bottom lip down the middle.
"Dammit!" I whisper as I lick blood from my lip.

I drop the picture of him beside my alarm clock, reach into the drawer again and find the tangerine treatment hiding under a love drenched card my husband gave me.

I think about love resting on the slippery surface of lip gloss, hoping it hadn't stained the words and how it had survived over the years beside me in a wooden drawer. As if it were just yesterday. A small piece of time from where we are today.

The lip gloss smooths away the blood and the cracks. I put the lid back on the container, reach down for my house coat resting on the floor beside the bed and drop the lip gloss in the pocket. I'm sure something will have to be smoothed over in the morning, including my lips.
I inhale the soft smell of oranges, look at the image of him one more time and turn off the light.

The darkness wraps around me. I blink my eyes to adjust to the darkness and stare into nothing and everything.

It's not fair.

My eyes are heavy with the burden of universal justice, oranges and the weight of tomorrow.

I sleep, but I don't dream. Not on that night.

Morning greets me with a blast from my ten-dollar alarm clock. It's not perfect, nor friendly, but it does the trick.

My husband rolls over, reaches his tired, muscular arm over my chest and with one swift movement, pulls me close to his body. We touch.

This is my favourite part of every morning. The part where his braided muscles fit all the way down the soft curves of my body. We are two puzzle pieces, missing for so many years, finally found and now fitting together perfectly every morning.

He loves me.

Our morning embrace fuels my long days with his heartbeat against my back, his breath on my neck, his arm over my breasts and our hands clasped in front of my heart.

It's time.
We untangle our bodies and feel the day press against us as we sit up and search the morning light for items of clothing.

Me: house coat, bathroom, toilet, teeth, face cloth, lip gloss. Coffee then kids.

He wanders into the kitchen pulling his sweatshirt over his head.
"What's with the picture of him?" he asks.
Before I can grasp any form of an answer, he says, "You really should go see him."
"I know," I quietly respond, "I know."

What I know is a far cry from what I should do. What I can do or what I want to do.
I wish the reality we face was just another one of his jokes.
Something we could laugh off.

A deep pain travels through my body. Deep, hard pain as strong as my husband's love, but opposite, awful, tenacious and real. Pain that doesn't go away when buttering toast, cleaning floors or crying saltwater tears into a sink full of dishes. It is always there hiding behind my child's perfect spelling test stuck to the fridge, or behind an orange peel scored for easy removal by my two girls and their small hands at lunch time in the classroom seventeen minutes away from me.

He is dying.

The phone call was as ordinary as a nine to five bankers' day (minus a robbery). My best friend called. It was one or two, maybe three lines at the end of a happy conversation preceded by, "Oh, by the way...did you hear?"
No.
No I hadn't heard.
I hadn't heard even though I had seen him at the Bryan Adams concert with his pregnant wife due any day with their second child.
I hadn't heard even though he and I stood on the street corner outside the bank where he was signing papers for their first mortgage on their first house.
He didn't tell me.
He left unhappy things and bad news for others to tell. As usual, we had laughed both those times.
We laughed, smiled, chatted and then hugged before we parted ways.

We hugged.

He always knew how to do that too. His hugs were more like taught string wrapping around his captive, trapping you in his merciless joy and camaraderie. You couldn't help but love him like a brother. He hugged like one too.

And we did, we all did. We loved him. Still do, but it is so much harder now. At least for me, yah, for me...it is so hard. Not the love part, but the going part.

All this feeling sorry for myself is making me sick. I've got to get past the luxury of time and feeling sorry for what I won't have. I've got to get past the excuses, the fabricated obstacles of a busy life, no time, bad weather and getting down my list of things to do in the grocery store.

I've got to stop.

Just stop like a small moment to put on lip gloss.

But it won't stop anything, it won't heal, smooth over or protect. The damage was done somewhere that is lost in an answer science is trying to retrieve from cells, plants, tissue, genetic code and deaths. Deaths linked together one at a time by a simple acronym that identifies the thief.

Treasures of muscles, signals, genetic code and a whole bunch of tomorrows, stolen and robbed while making breakfast when the knife is dropped for no particular reason and you don't know why.

Treasures robbed by an arm twitch that mysteriously appears and spreads. Speech slurring like a drunken fool wandering down the street, wobbly, staggering here and there then landing in a wheelchair and never getting up.

Not for anyone ever again.

It's a red wheelchair. Good as they come, just like him. He operates it by a hand control. It hasn't totally stolen hand movement yet, but they say at some point it will.

I don't know what is worse, having warning or not.

Would I want to know that in two year's time, I'm going to die? Or is it better to die sailing through the air on your last snowmobile ride into the night and off a cliff with a friend holding on tight, falling down six hundred meters to a snow covered rock ledge, but not enough snow to break your fall then wait for the helicopter to retrieve you and your friend's body lying too far away for your Mother to kiss you goodnight or goodbye.

Or is it better to be on your way home to your baby girl, your girlfriend and your first house with droopy eyes from a long

night at work driving into the ditch as your eyes close for the
last time because of the tidy tank in the back of your truck that
couldn't stop when your truck did in the ditch.

How would you like to die?

The loss, the loss, the loss, oh the loss we have felt from the
cliff and the ditch. Crying at the funerals.

There have been others, many more friends and family that
have traveled to the place you are headed, but they didn't have
any warning even though we still cried at their funerals.
Not like you sitting in your wheelchair watching the red lights
flashing from an imaginary place in my mind, warning you of
danger, one more muscle gone, not working
or responding to your brain which is very much alive. The
warning lights flash.
Danger, danger, danger, around in circles lighting up behind
you like a campfire in a dark place with nothing for you to
stand on.

Nobody is laughing now.

I doubled over in pain after that phone call with my best friend.
I laid on the floor sobbing like I did for my mother when she
had cancer and the drugs wracked her body.

I lay helpless on the floor, controlled by the loneliness of a beautiful spirit trapped like a demon in a virgin's body fornicating on the steps of a church screaming "no." We never worshiped any gods. Only the laughter of our friends summoned by your quick wit and smooth deliverance. The coy looks of characters bursting through your lips, your eyes and into the cool night air.

We were free back then on the beach with shiny futures.

I called your mom after that phone call that started it all.
She was full of hope even though it was true.
She was optimistic and asked me to be strong for you.
You get your grace from her. She is always smiling, looking at the bright side, ready to be adopted by the next lost soul, but never putting up with anyone's disrespect.

She was our mother too.
Full of hugs, wise words and support for a group of wily teenagers searching the night for identity, respect and love.
She was always there in the morning, in the sunshine weekends with our frosty breath in the back yard with the animals, teaching us about life one moment at a time.
I still feel like a teenager when she is near.
Your mom, our mother.

Then I phoned you.
I had to wait a few days to collect myself and practice what I would say. I checked my tool kit of words, picked all the

right ones and set to work placing them together like a piece of wooden furniture.

I never finished that project.

I just picked up the phone and called.

I ended up saying something mundane and straight to the point. I asked why you didn't tell me at the concert or on the street corner in the sunshine when I talked about health. When I said we both had learned that you have nothing if you don't have your health.

Why didn't you tell me then?

Why didn't you tell me before I rambled on about cancer, death, illness and how lucky we were not to be faced with those burdens.
I said those words on the street corner outside the bank, words that have haunted me ever since,

"You have nothing if you don't have your health."

I wish lip gloss and time could heal the blunder on my lips as you stood there on the corner with a fresh diagnosis and the acronym ALS running through your head.

I'm sorry.

I'm sorry for so many things that I can't write them all on a page, but somehow this has to go on.

I'm sorry you are dying.

I'm sorry you won't be here to sit on a park bench at eighty-five holding your wife's hand, feeding the pigeons.

I'm sorry your two rough and tumble boys at four and six have to watch you fade away.

One day you can hug, the next day you can't. Not ever again. Not even for them.

It's all such a waste. My heart beats and I can't give you anything to make you stay.

I can't go to war for you to retrieve all the spent muscles that have traveled so far away to foreign beaches, lost in the sand.

I can't search the night anymore with laughter and warning lights.

I can't even visit you. It just hurts too much.

But, I won't forget you.

Not ever.

When you are gently laid down tonight with your thin skin draped over your skeleton frame resting on the bed beside your wife with all the particular pieces of life pulling at you, I will dream.

I will dream of your long muscular body fitting neatly into soft curves of the girl you married.

I will dream of the characters that fit neatly into our lives on the beach.

I will dream of laughter, small hands, your boys and oranges.

I will dream of their future with their mother and no father

I will dream of love.

And in the night, I will wish you could forever smell oranges, feel the weight of tomorrow and hear the sound of a ten-dollar alarm clock in the morning.

After her son died

In the garden
I found you
weeping
Sweets sobs of mercy
I dropped
And on my knees
I wept
with you
Our sober embrace of tears
haunts me
And as you faded
into the night
I prayed
that one day I would hold you again
And I stayed
weeping
in the garden

Funeral Shoes

She is standing on the stairs
searching
for the next step
through
welled up tears
As she looks down
her heartache
drips down
tear
by
tear
onto her shiny shoes
Funeral shoes
The ones tucked away
for
special occasions
the ones you carry
band aids
for
blisters
rubbed raw
This is an occasion
but not
special
You were
And all of your
twelve years
Now she must step

Down
Down
Down
those dreadful
horrible
stairs
Down
to the path
Down
to the car
Down
to your body
that waits
to be
lowered
down
Into the earth
Where she will
see you no more
This one
step
she must take
with her shiny shoes
with tears that will not stop
with band aids for blisters
without
you
Down she must go

As must you
But, she cannot move
She cannot step
down
from being your mother
from trying to save you
from the cancer
She cannot admit defeat
Nor the desperate cry from your brother
as he begged you
to stay
to not die
to not leave him
to not
leave
us
Yet, there she is
at the top of the stairs
searching
for so many things
for changes she cannot make
for everything, something and nothing
for one more curse to a god that would not listen
for something that might be a reason

to take the next step
in funeral shoes
for the loss
of something
special
on this occasion

After her daughter died

When the sun sets
and I'm alone in my thoughts
I think of you. The love I have known from you
is the place where I want to stay
But you are gone
The sun is setting
and all I know how to be is alone.

I reach for you in the dead of night and you're not there
I cry and I'm scared

Where have you gone and why have you left me?

It was not that long ago that you were my baby
It was not that long ago that you were my child

And as I fade from myself in the dark days of tomorrow
I wish to hold you one more time

I see you in my dreams
that is why I crave the night
But that too is fading
And I want the light to dim
so I can't see my crying eyes
so I can't see the memories that surround me

And one day
I will evaporate into the place I lost you to

I hope you are safe there
I hope you are loved there
I hope to see you soon

Until then
I'll be alone in my thoughts
watching the sun set
and thinking of you

Maddy

In the middle of the ring
she's holding a string
attached to every dog's heart

There she stands

in Heaven

It's not where we want her
to be
but she stands strong
happy
holding a string

And the rays shine down
the sparkle of her soul

Catches the light

At dawn

When we wake and show
When we do our go rounds
When we meet in the ring

Holding a string
To every dog's heart

She's in the middle of the ring
Not where we want her to be

But, in Heaven.

Stevie

I have to put you down
I hope that is ok
I have carried you long enough
until you would be old enough to die

It's been a long journey
between you and I
and I'm sorry

My drive for perfection
outweighed
what was right
what honored you
and me

We both suffered
in different ways
different times
But it was all
so horrible

Watching you in pain
Your breath racing
Your eyes closed
because…
because of the pain

it
was
unbearable
and I had
nothing
to help you
but to let you go

and I fell to the floor
when you sighed
breathing your last
big
beautiful
breath

I was gutted
All my dreams
died
with you

And the holes
in our lives
made no sense
just a haze of anger
and hate

for all the things that should have gone right

You died too soon
Too young
for no good reason

So I carried you
everywhere
to vindicate you
remember you
keep you close to
my heart
to try
and forgive myself
for putting
my dreams first, myself first
and not you

I'm not sure
if I'm there at forgiveness
but what I've realized
is that
holding onto you
keeps us in the pain
and hate

You've suffered long enough
So
I have to put you down
I hope that is ok

Prognosis

In the morning
she will be dead
No more days will pass by for her
She will rise up
indifferent
Past all her sorrows and troubles
Up and away
beyond what held her here

The shallow breath
of death
will haunt them
The waiting, waiting, waiting
for the release
The peace
and the sorrow to begin

For JSN

Of all the things
it is today
I want

But I yearn for tomorrow
when things
will be better

And as I long
for the sun and moon
to change places

I know that wanting tomorrow
more than
today
is
missing the mark
of this moment

When I die

I was never what I do
It's who I am
that's gone

Honour the body that served me
A mere vehicle
to teach me

Lay it on crisp linen
with flowers
and petals
Wash it clean
with
or without
tears

It served me well
so honour it
Thank it
Trust that all it was
Will go back
to dust

But I will live on
The body is not myself

I will miss you
for as long as I can
One fleeting moment
and no more

We are always
together
on bended light

In the same space that
calls my name

Walk away from
the body
resting and beautiful

For
I am
Always
No matter what
I do.

PART FIVE

Becoming a mother was like opening a door of emotions that can't be closed.

I was young, inexperienced, but determined and to a degree, stubborn. I had to make it work, there was no other way. What I didn't realize is how the changing title of 'mother' would shape me and determine how I was defined by others. How I would be rejected, accepted and loved.

But, I had to keep going. Holding onto love, giving everything I could and praying that someday they all would understand.

And *if I were to say something about it,* these would be the words of my journey as a mother.

My Mercy

I open the door and peek in her bedroom, looking at her now, sleeping, so innocent, it's hard to believe she was once a small child. She still breathes the soft, restful breaths of infancy, but piled on top of her are layers of life lessons, experiences and hesitations of leaving childhood.

My baby is growing up.

It wasn't that long ago she arrived in a style all her own. Born on a Wednesday night, in no hurry to make head way, but knowing, eventually, she would make it from the warmth of my womb, into my arms.

She made her own way out, on her terms.

There she was, a bit hesitant to breathe too quickly or cry too hard, just content to be here, in the world and take in the activity around her.

Very quickly, she became my reason. For so many things I can't even name. A pull as strong as survival and breathing. My life at 20 years was just beginning. So was motherhood. And for her, childhood. We were in this together, like it or not.

I'm not sure what the master plan was then. Heck, I was just having fun and got caught. I think about that now. I think about what my life would have been without her. But really, it's unimaginable – all these years of thick memories. Love, birth, separation, pain and back to love. She was there through it all. She shaped the parts of me I am most proud of.

A mother formed out of dimples, little hands, girl dreams, whispers and soft touches.

I named her Mercedes, Spanish for "merciful." She has grown into her name more and more every year.
She was such an easy child, always happy. I'd often find her in gumboots and a diaper, reading a book in the sunlight. She always managed to find the rays of sunshine that broke through the dark moments of our lives.

I'm in a plane flying across the Prairies, looking out the window at the vastness of the land. I wish she was here to see how big the spaces are from up so high. I wish she could see that life doesn't end at the edge of a small city. It's big like an idea that stretches across the minds of many people.
This year is the start of a new journey for her. Graduation. Grade 12 and beyond.
I want to hold onto her, hold her tight like the first day of kindergarten when the big yellow bus swallowed her up and drove away.
The welling up of tears is that of both pride and sadness. I can't hold on forever, but it seems that 18 years were not enough.
When she was little, I couldn't wait. Couldn't wait until she ate solid food or spoke her first word. Her first sentence, her first step, her first day of school, her first report card, her first loose tooth, her first best friend, her first crush, her first

sleepover, her first kiss, her first boyfriend, her first car.

Now, looking back, I feel like I rushed it. Pushed too hard. Lived more in the excitement of the future than the satisfaction of the now. The present.

She was my gift. And, as I cling to the final moments of now, I know I must face my hardest first with her.

Letting go.

Letting go of having a say, holding her hand and protecting her from the big world ready to swallow her up. I realize the sharp reality that she will always have me, but I may not always have her.

A mother's love is sometimes a mother's greatest sorrow.

I'm not in a rush these days, even though her graduation is only a few weeks away. I'm content to wait, savor the soft restful breaths she breathes. The now.

I hope in all the confusion of our days together, in all the directions a single mother gets pulled, that some way, somehow, I have given her enough.

If nothing else, I hope she walks out the door knowing she was loved in ways words will never find, appreciated for her soft touch on my life and the way her 18 years have shaped me.

She's getting ready to leave for school. I worry and fuss over her. (Does she know it's cold out? Does she have a jacket? Did she make a lunch?) I catch myself and pull back.

She's 18 and I've got to let go.

I hear her car start and rush out the door with her lunch before she pulls away. There in the window, I see a reflection of me – I hesitate and look through the reflection at her in the driver's seat.
She rolls down the window, I hand her, her lunch.

"Thanks mom, love you," she says. I smile and wave as she drives away.

Walking up the stairs, I grab my book and stand for a moment in the warm rays of sunshine streaming through the window. And, softly, I whisper to myself, "No, thank you Mercedes, thank you."

I open my book, turn the page and start a new chapter.

Guilt

After a heavy, "I love you," at the airport, two lost weeks
amongst the shadows and numb souls, I told him, "I'm leaving
you."

But you told him you loved him.
But the children.
But the house, the dog, the car, the boat, the friends.

I'm leaving.

The heavy burden of five years melted away in one phone call.
In three words, my spirit started to glow again. The days I had
spent on my knees praying, crying, begging for the strength to
keep going.

For the sake of the children.
For the sake of the marriage.
For the sake of the family.
In the name of God.

I was born into the thick flesh of religion. A bastard child
hidden and given away.

For the sake of the child.
To save face.
Because she was told it was best.
Because it was what love looked like back then.

Or so we were told.

But, I'm leaving.

I'm tearing our family apart. I'm taking the girls. I'm taking them both. I'm taking the dog.
We will live at my mother's house.
The rest. Besides a few possessions.
We leave behind.

It's easy to say. Leave Behind.
But, at church. I hear them talking. About evil, about shame, about breaking God's promise, his covenant between two people.
I broke it and I feel them stare. The penetrating look of repentance, of justice, of looking back and watching me turn to salt.
None have bent down to see my blistered and burnt feet from my trip through hell. My fractured heart strings, the whip marks on my spirit. Do they not see my stooped posture? A burden so heavy only a mother could carry.
The blood.
The blood and tearing of birth once and then twice, was not enough penance for all of us, for me. The wounds were just a beginning.

Every day my heart rests on sharpened blades endlessly pulled between the past and the future. Only 'right now' saves me from doubting. But, I lean against this sturdy emotion, the one that makes me cripple when I have to say no. It's my fault and only I should pay. Pay the price of broken love. Fix the tiny pieces with the glue of yes. The never-ending bond to the past. The one so sticky, moving on means releasing myself from the web of lies, of long nights and tears that turn to blood. The unholy days of raising children from a bastard mother, dragged through pain, weighted with dignity, lifted by pride and kept going by sheer tenacity and the hope that tomorrow will bring a hint of relief. Just a hint. It's all one needs to take the next step away from the ledge, to put two pills back and drink one less glass of sanity. It's all one needs, just enough hope to say no, to say okay, to be semi-conscious in a scowling world that sets tables for four and carnival rides for two.

We are three.
A Mother.
A child.
Another child.
Three.

No father that one can see, invisible, vacant and lost. Lost in the past and trapped in the days of playmates, school yards and the comfort of a mother's care. Nothing solid, just empty ground, slopes to slide down and tender kisses that will never come from his mother again.
It's about growing up. Leaving the nursery. Lost boys forever. With nothing but red cherry juice stains and giggles.
Boys.
Boys left haunted by the memories of yesterday.
Boys, I left behind.
The one I left with an empty, "I love you."

It was in the days after the plane lifted off, my dad drove me away with two kids, one dog and endless pain that it began to seep in.

Every word I spoke sounded like I'm sorry. Sounded hollow, gaunt, robbed of nutrition, deprived of love.

It poisoned the Christmas concerts, as I sat there as one mother with an empty chair beside her, watching two children on stage, desperately trying to shield them from their past, hoping the stage lights would brighten their future. Even if it was only a song about Christmas, I wanted the darkness of my decision to leave a little flicker of hope for their tomorrow.

But it never seemed easy.

Their deep longing eyes begging for the reason behind the number one. When all I had for them was a riddle about how numbers get broken.

It almost crushed me to death when she asked me – mommy, will you ever divorce me?

Riddles are not to be played with or read as bedtime stories, dressed in footie pajamas and tucked in until next year. Especially ones about broken numbers.

It goes on and on – unsolvable, unwavering and full of pain.

It never stops.

Settled like a heavy mist on the love I give, it's a distance I can't travel from yes to no.

And, I'm guilty of every decision, of every pain, of every teardrop on the kitchen table set for three.

It's the burden of guilt that I lean against as I say, I love you, as I kiss them goodbye, as I look back and watch them turn to salt and fall into the never ending wound of separation, constantly pulled between a lost boy and a mother left bleeding, influenced by the dark shadow of raging guilt that turns into yes, when the answer should be no and carries me to a violent freedom with all the scars of my decision on my soul.

And, a number that equals one.

p.s. I love you.

Losing definition

It's a quiet Thursday afternoon.
She is sitting across the room from me sipping her tea.
Slowly, with her good arm, she raises the cup to her lips and
takes a gentle sip. Then, with a little tremble in her arm, lowers
the cup down and sets it victoriously on the table.
She has come home – this is her welcome: tea. A satisfying, yet
challenging cup of tea. But, true to my mother's style, she
doesn't complain and smiles – she says she is fine.

She is far from that ringing word 'fine'.
Fine is what you are after you stub your toe; she has cancer –
she is not fine.
I wish she would scream or crumple into a helpless heap,
anything but sit there and be fine because I can't deal with fine.
She is not, we are not and perhaps will never again be the
definition of that word 'fine'.

I can't help myself as I keep staring at her afflicted breasts.
I feel guilty gawking at them, shifting my eyes from one side of
her chest to the other. I'm looking carefully to see a difference.
I'm looking to see how much the surgery has changed them.
I'm wondering how she feels about them now.
I'm remembering how I felt about them before the cancer.

My mother's breasts were a childhood fascination for me. They
were large and full, bursting out of her bra. They shaped her
clothes and made her shirts pull in all the right places. They
were what mother's breasts should be and I loved them.

I was never breast-fed as a child – I was adopted – yet, I still claimed them and unknowingly fostered a love affair with them. Those wonderful breasts were my model of attained womanhood. One day, I too would have those big breasts. Big, soft, full, beautiful mother breasts were my fantasy. Until then, I had mom's and as a child I enjoyed them.

I remember in my childhood how I would nestle myself into her lap and lay my head against her chest on those wonderful breasts. I would poke them and push them with my hands all the while feeling their softness with my head. They were flesh pillows. They were mine.

As I got a little older, I got meaner. My expectations in my eighth year had become my downfall – I didn't yet have those breasts – why? I remember lashing out one day and hitting mother on the breast. She winced.
I remember her telling me how I had hurt her.
I believed her, but only just a little, so I hit her again just to make sure that breasts had feeling.
Just to make sure.

But now being sure has taken on new meaning in the throes of surgeries and treatments.
The first time she had cancer we were shocked, but sure.
It was lymphoma.
It was low grade.
It was treatable.

We were treatable and my mother was going to be safe after a few pills.

It is different this time.

It has taken ahold of her breasts. I can see them, they are on her chest expressing a vibrant aspect of her feminine make up. I couldn't see lymph nodes. Of all her body parts, why her breasts? Her beautiful breasts.

One long month has gone by and my mother is reaching for the clean pajamas I extend towards her. The chemo started today and so did the vomiting. Just a few hours ago, I witnessed a red chemical transfer from a syringe into my mother's arm. Then a clear one. Then a milky one.

Apparently, they are working, they have possessed my mother's body and she is out of control. The retching is violent. It's far beyond any Saturday morning hangover. There is nothing to do, nothing I can do, but stand back and watch.

As I help her into the warm, blue top of her pj's, I look at her breast. The cause of all the ruckus tonight. The nipple is skewed. It doesn't know where it is going, or which way to go. Neither do I. Here in my mother's bedroom, in the darkness, I am in the centre of womanhood. I am thirty years old. I am mothering my mother and I am lost.

Like my mother's breast, her poor distorted breast, we are trying to be 'normal' and untouched by cancer.

But, her breast is not, she is not, we are not.

We all have been violated.

I am beginning to feel like a part of the surgical wounds on my mother's breast. Like I'm sinking into the tissue, embedded, trapped and I'm living in cancer.

As the week goes on, she gains strength and the vomiting stops.
When I visit, she moves slowly from bed to couch. She likes to have a reason to get out of bed. I'm her reason some days. Other days, I think it is sheer will, her genetic determination. I watch her move about the house. She moves with that inherited determination and a little defiance.
Today, she is making a thank you card.
Her eyes have been affected by the chemo, so she has to bend close to the table to see what she is doing. It makes the red scarf on her head slip forward and she gives it a well-rehearsed adjustment. She says it's just one of those things you have to deal with – you can't fuss over such trivial things as hair loss. She goes back to making her card because she has many things to be thankful for.
And she is.

She phoned today – to see if I was okay – to check on me. I lied. I have to lie. Every day it is a lie.
"I'm okay Mom."
I speak those words to protect her and to some degree, protect myself. These days, we are all living precariously. I know there are days when saying the words, "I'm okay," stops me from screaming. Stops me from venturing into a delicious

insanity where I can vent the truth.

We are not okay.

My mother is not okay.

The cancer is spreading and now I have it. It is in my mind, in my thoughts and today, it reached my heart.

The sun was shining today, but I didn't see it. I didn't feel it.

Mom…are we going to die?

Every three weeks she visits the hospital. It is usually on a Tuesday.

Tuesdays are chemo days and I wear a red scarf on my head. I have hair and for now, I have my mother. The red scarf is my strength. I wear it because it is all I have. It is all I can do as a gesture of support and it is one thing that my Mother and I share.

At least today it is.

And, I sit beside her as yet another chemo treatment begins.

My hand trembles just a little as I sip gently at a cup of tea and watch the red fade into my mother's arm.

The Terrifying Mother

"You are nothing but a piece of worthless shit."
Those words rattle around in my head
I don't like them
But
they serve a purpose.

The days are heavy
everything seems like an uphill climb
Running into unmet expectations in the form of pointed
questions
seems to be the new way to greet me.
Why didn't you do this? Why didn't you do that?
You should.
You could.
You can't.
I won't.

And it's not even the men that irk me as much
it's the women
the passive looks
The way they choose their words that are so telling
of how they see me as a woman without a husband
with children
Things like, "Oh that's so terrible."
When what they really mean is
"I'm glad it's not me."
The distance they create
because divorce might be contagious.

"When are you going to stop talking about all this?"
I was asked.
Like, do you mean talking about all the heaviness?
The hate?
The lies?
The leaving?

The words of a very pointed question laced with a quiet reality
that they too were just one misstep away from leaving.
But let's not be too silly
or carried away
talking to me is as close to separation from their luxury car as
they want to get.

I'm all the things they are afraid of. When I talk about it all.

I was never looking for champagne flutes of pity
or the one hundred percent fault that was hoisted on me
by them
I didn't work for their glancing looks and painted words
("She left him, those poor children.")

All I ever did was nothing they could do.

I left.

because I had to. because I couldn't be someone's worthless
piece of shit.

And then,
I was just trying to be a mother
without a man, without a marriage.
Isn't that what it is anyway?

But you quickly learn how horrible you really are
Without a man
Without a marriage
Without the license from a god
to be a mother

You never will meet their expectations
not because you didn't try (god knows you did)
but because they are not expectations
at all
They are all the things they go to confession for
Their desires
Their jealousy
An embarrassing wish
to be as terrifying as you are
just
being undefined
brave
single
and
a mother

Motherhood

From the moment I knew they were there
Inside me
The first butterfly wing flutters that said, I am here.
The smile that filled my body when I felt them move
The senses no one would know, but me
The pureness of the journey alone and together

I'm transported to that joy every time I see them
The softness that touched me inside
One but not the same
A blurry two with one body housing a great miracle

And I never saw them as me
But as me doing something for them
Nourishing, sacrificing, growing, loving
Protecting
All the pains of nine months
The anticipation
of birth

Your body is not yours then
It is being governed by something greater
as it contracts and heaves, hurts and tears
It's giving, giving, giving
And your mind wanders in the pain
But somehow you know
Somewhere you draw a great strength
that only you are privy to
To keep going

Light and dark, flashes of despair
Flashes of pain
Your body is gripped by everything and nothing
It is donated to them
A lending out of flesh and the end of your journey together
as one body
birthing the miracle

I had no awareness of them
Of their journey through me
Only the pain and the searing heat of the tears that needed to
happen
to get them out
to ensure one was not sacrificed for the other
One body ripping apart
for another
And then it's over
They are free of you with head and shoulders leading the way
With the sharpness of scissors
And the very first cry

Free

They begin and you end.

And in that moment of separation, little did I know it is the
beginning of a great journey of grieving
Of not being able to go back
Not being able to get back what you gave

But not regretting it
I think it is more about what only you know
The singular feelings that are impossible to share
The sadness that the beginning of motherhood
is the end

I have spent a lifetime worrying they will leave me
A lifetime of giving without any thought of getting something
back
An expectation of love and respect
but a payback, no

I had hopes as big as the Universe for their little hands and feet
for their futures that had no marks
Only potential
What I could give them in a few short years

The tough days are the ones when I look back
through the lens of my fifty years of living
What I could have done, what I tried to do
What I traded in desperation
on a theory
that the deals I was making were for a better future
when where I was standing had no hope for a tomorrow

So where does motherhood end?

Like the rhythmic breathing
the deep breath in and out
It's a vacillation between joy and pain
A lifetime of ache
A place of swirling emotion that can't be cut away
with sharp scissors

I may never know a true definition of where I end and they
begin
regardless of how hard we all try
I am governed by something greater that brought them to this
place
And although they may walk alone, separate from me
there is something visceral that can't be undone from all the
breaths I took for them

And so you ask me to leave you alone
To stop being your mother
To let you be

Because you have asked me
I will try
It is as easy as undoing my life
and yours

As I head towards death as each year passes
As I become more aware of the time I don't have
There will never be a day I won't be your mother
as you now know me

Even when my body has been burned and put in the ground
I will always be your mother
When the soft winds blow your curtains in the morning and you
breathe in the warm air
when the rays of the sun warm your face
when you hold a small hand
Those things will forever be me
I will never end being a part of you
I will never be an other
or a separate part
of an impossible equation that untangles us
For you see, no matter how hard we try, the one thing you
cannot get away from is the flesh of who you are, the deep code
I gave you that you cannot cleanse out of your system
A deep code that continues from one generation to the next
And a love that never ends
With me
Or we

Love, your mother.

PART SIX

I have always been a fighter, a survivor, a thriver. Loyal, strong.
Until I couldn't fight anymore.
Until I had to make a choice.

I am forever grateful...for so many things. Without them I would not be here.

I'm ok. More than I have ever been.

Keep going. Look for the silver lining. It will all be ok.

And *if I were to say something about it*, these are the words of complete surrender in the moment I chose me.

On the third ring of my third attempt, he answered in a crowded room. The hustle and clinking of Friday night drinks and social libations competed with the words that tumbled out of me as I stood on the beach under the pale moonlight, waves crashing and a million grains of sand shifting under the weight of what I needed to say before the weekend.

"It's time for me to take a new path."

There was an unhinged feeling, an irreverence in the air as the words drifted between us, countries apart.

"This makes me sad" he said.

"Me too."

Earlier in the day he had promised to take care of me.

What wasn't mistakable is that is exactly why I was leaving – because had I been taken care of over the last thirteen and a half years, I would have stayed.

But, that's not really the point.

The point is that I was drifting away with the growing tides of self-worth, understanding and intolerance.

Once you see, there is no turning back. Not that I wanted to, or that I even could since the words were free of me, but just knowing the small details, the thin fractures that became the obvious reasons, it just becomes so much easier to drop your life off the balcony and watch it shatter.

It felt like the relief after vomiting. Still sick, but the poison expelled. The nausea had been with me for well over a year, perhaps two, but it was really the last few months that I had really been affected by it. I'd been staving it off with excuses, ignoring the bad behavior, the vileness of a loyalty between men that had no place for the sensibilities, fairness and empathy of a woman. And it was getting worse each day.

I despise bullies, probably because I had been prone to flirting with the drivers of jealousy and hate until Terri-Lynn confronted me in grade six. Child's play, mean comments because I wanted something they had and, in all probability, I was again. Jealous. That I didn't have it in me to be ruthless, to create fear in everyone around me veiled as respect. I cared. I cared about those who were being kicked despite their earnest efforts. It was the twisted logic, the comfort they didn't want to disrupt and the emblazoned egos that refused to see the cold, hard facts that were excused because saving your own ass is all that mattered.

And so, I quit.

I stepped up to the railing of my third floor, rented condo in Mexico, looked out over the ocean and watched all I had built in my career free fall to the ground. I looked down and wanted nothing of the scattered shards exploded on the ground below me. I had let go, and they had too.

I was free. And, in every definition, alone. They didn't want to save me. They didn't say, "No, you can't go," or "No, you have to stay." Those words are reserved for the boys Terri-Lynn didn't get to talk to in grade six. The ones who kicked puppies because no one would pick them first for their team in gym class. Saving was reserved for those who were picked on. Protected by positions, titles and festering childhood wounds that still chased them after school. Revenge against girls who said no, when they asked. When the comfort of code protected them from active humanity. Their firewall from forgiveness. No one stood in the way of their insecurities, monthly subscriptions of power trips, egos and inadequacies that were obvious to everyone except those who could do something about it.

So, I quit.

There was no longer a need to prove myself to a trove of men who could not see the value of a woman speaking the truth. Pointing out problems. Their flaws and what should be done.

What I was guilty of was not understanding the elixir of power and vengeance. It's like whiskey and syrup, a mixture that provides a slow, sweet burn from head to toe. It's dangerous because you can have too much. And they did. Drunk with desire of having your way and none other, settling scores.

I could not witness their wanton diet of empty calories of sweetness and poison and how it terrorized the tender hearted, the timid, the ones too scared to say their good idea.

How it terrorized the women because they saw how they went after me.

I had fought a one-woman war for so long.

I had said my piece. And they didn't listen.

They tried to hear, sort of, but it was more a placation of their soul and not of my pain, my worry or concern of where we were headed.

And it was in all those little moments. All those empty promises. All those years of struggle to get to the top. In all of it, it came down to one moment in the darkness on a beach in Mexico.

That I quit…them.

I had spent my years thinking I was doing something good, something right, something greater than myself and as I stood there listening to the waves crash, I realized I had suffered my own kind of poison. One part righteousness, one part silence, one part desperation and one part love. When mixed properly, it made me believe that all the moments I had been there had made a difference. It made me dismiss the inequity, the vile words, the inappropriate touches, comments and actions. It made me believe I was not worth it, but that others were.

And after I hung up and the libations continued a country away, I took a deep breath of freedom. It was my final test. And I had passed. It was the moment that I finally mattered.

The one-woman war was over and I was free.

As the sun rose and the little shard of things that had been dropped sparkled on the concrete, I too rose up and walked bare foot to the ocean and let the salt-water cleanse my soul. I let everything, everyone and them had wanted, their codes and grins drift away on the tide. I yearned for the waves to crash over me, but I was too tender and beautiful in this moment of just been born in the morning on the first day of being me. After I quit.

ABOUT THE AUTHOR

STEFANIE GIDDENS is a writer, former tech executive, and award-winning business leader. She has always been a passionate advocate for women, helping them find their voices, speak their truth, and stand up against daily injustices.

Throughout her career, she has had the privilege of working alongside many incredible women, leading, learning from, and being continually inspired by them to keep going.

Her work, marked by raw authenticity and deep emotional resonance, is intended to connect, empower, and encourage women to keep going, love themselves, and let past experiences shape resilience, not limit potential.

Stefanie holds a Bachelor of Journalism and an Associate of Arts degree from Thompson Rivers University, along with numerous professional certifications. Her debut book of poetry, *If I were to say something about it,* reflects on pivotal moments in her life and experiences as a woman, celebrating the resilience and strength it takes to navigate life's challenges and to truly find love and self-worth.

Healing is a journey, and her hope is that her words find those looking for a message that they will be ok. Keep going.

For more information, or to book Stefanie for speaking engagements, please visit tlbirch.com.

Instagram: @writingbystefanie

ACKNOWLEDGMENTS

There are so many people past and present that have supported
me, inspired me and helped me make this book a reality.
I am forever grateful.

The matriarchs on the other side, Gammy & Nana

My mom, my rock, my everything, Elizabeth
My daughters, Mercedes & Makayla

My #1 fan, my love, Chris

My lifelong soul sister, Laura
My lifeline, coach and friend, Heather

My Aunt Nancy for being an artist and always being in my
corner

The one who gave me life, Kim

For all your sunshine and love, Momma Sue

All the amazing women I had the honour to lead and work
side-by-side with
There are many, but to name a few:
Richelle | Pavan | Darcy | Candus | Veronika | Rebekka | Caity
Marion | Lisa G | Nan | Jolanda | Avi | Tammy | Ginny | Lauren
Shelley

For my photo shoot 'signature look', Julie Skinner of JS Signature Style

For glamming me up with your amazing talents - hair styling, makeup artistry and on-site styling, Rebecca 'Becca' Lafleur of Blank Canvas Beauty Collective

For guiding me through the process, all your valuable insights, experience and encouragement, and for being so patient with me, Jennifer Sparks of STOKE Publishing

The one person who can truly capture me in an image, who I wholeheartedly trust with a camera and who took such care and attention to get the right images for this book and who willingly bussed across Canada with me, the one and only Darren Hull

Mike H, if you know, you know

Dr. Rachel Nash, you will always be my A+ and I wish you were here to see what you inspired in these pages

Dr. Kate Sutherland, without your teaching, I would never have found my love for literature

Dr. Maxine Ruvinsky, for being wonderfully fierce and for your amazing grammar classes

Ginny Ratsoy, for all the learning and laughter in your Canadian Literature classes

To the 'Sedona Group of Seven', from the bottom of my heart, thank you for seeing me and supporting me…it was the final piece to making this book happen

Manufactured by Amazon.ca
Bolton, ON